NATURE'S CYCLES

THE WATER CYCLE

A.B. CLAMANT

NorwoodHouse Press

Cataloging-in-Publication Data

Names: Clamant, A.B.
Title: The water cycle / A.B. Clamant.
Description: Buffalo, NY : Norwood House Press, 2026. | Series: Nature's cycles | Includes glossary and index.
Identifiers: ISBN 9781978575707 (pbk.) | ISBN 9781978575714 (library bound) | ISBN 9781978575721 (ebook)
Subjects: LCSH: Hydrologic cycle--Juvenile literature.
Classification: LCC GB848.C536 2026 | DDC 551.48--dc23

Published in 2026 by
Norwood House Press
2544 Clinton Street
Buffalo, NY 14224

Designer: Rhea Magaro
Editor: Kim Thompson

Photo credits: Cover, p. 1 Sven Hansche/Shutterstock.com; p. 3 ORION PRODUCTION/Shutterstock.com; p. 5 Ruslan Pobuta/Shutterstock.com; p. 6 kavram/Shutterstock.com; p. 7 nikkytok/Shutterstock.com; p. 9 MA. Turcotte/Shutterstock.com; pp. 10/11 gui jun peng/Shutterstock.com; p. 12 fortton/Shutterstock.com; p. 13 kajeab_pongsiri/Shutterstock.com; p. 15 Creatikon Studio/Shutterstock.com; p. 16 Olga Danylenko/Shutterstock.com; p. 17 John A. Anderson, P. 17 Shy Radar/Shutterstock.com; P. 17 Tahseenamjad/Shutterstock.com; p. 18 Nick Fox/Shutterstock.com; p. 19 Tatevosian Yana/Shutterstock.com; p. 20 denayunebgt/Shutterstock.com; p. 21 Mark Byer/Shutterstock.com

Printed in the United States of America

TABLE OF CONTENTS

What Is the Water Cycle?

Look around on a rainy day. There is water in the sky. There is water on the ground. Did you know that water goes back and forth between those two places? It goes around and around in a **cycle**.

Water Heats and Rises

The water cycle begins with the Sun. The Sun shines on oceans, rivers, lakes, and streams. The Sun's heat warms up the water.

When water gets hot, it turns from a liquid into a gas. It turns into tiny, invisible drops of water. This gas is called **water vapor**.

The process of heated water turning into water vapor is called **evaporation**.

During evaporation, water vapor rises into the sky.

Clouds Form

The higher water vapor rises, the cooler it gets. When water vapor cools down enough, it turns back into liquid water. This is called **condensation**.

Condensation causes clouds to form. Fog, dew, and droplets of water forming on a cold soda can also happen because of condensation.

Condensed droplets of water clump together high in the sky. They form clouds.

Wind blows clouds. They collect more and more water droplets. The clouds get bigger.

Water Falls

Water droplets join inside clouds. Clouds get heavier. When a cloud's drops get too heavy to float, they fall. This is called **precipitation**.

Most precipitation begins as snow high in the clouds. As snowflakes get closer to Earth, the air gets warmer. The snow melts and becomes raindrops.

Temperature and wind control what type of precipitation falls. In winter, the snow stays frozen all the way down to the ground. **Hail** and **sleet** are types of precipitation too.

The Cycle Continues

Precipitation falls to the ground. It fills up oceans, lakes, rivers, and streams. This is called **collection**.

The Sun heats up the water, and the water cycle starts again. Water gets recycled over and over. The water you drink today is over four billion years old!

Plants and animals need water. The water cycle makes life on Earth possible. With the Sun's help, Earth will continue this amazing cycle forever.

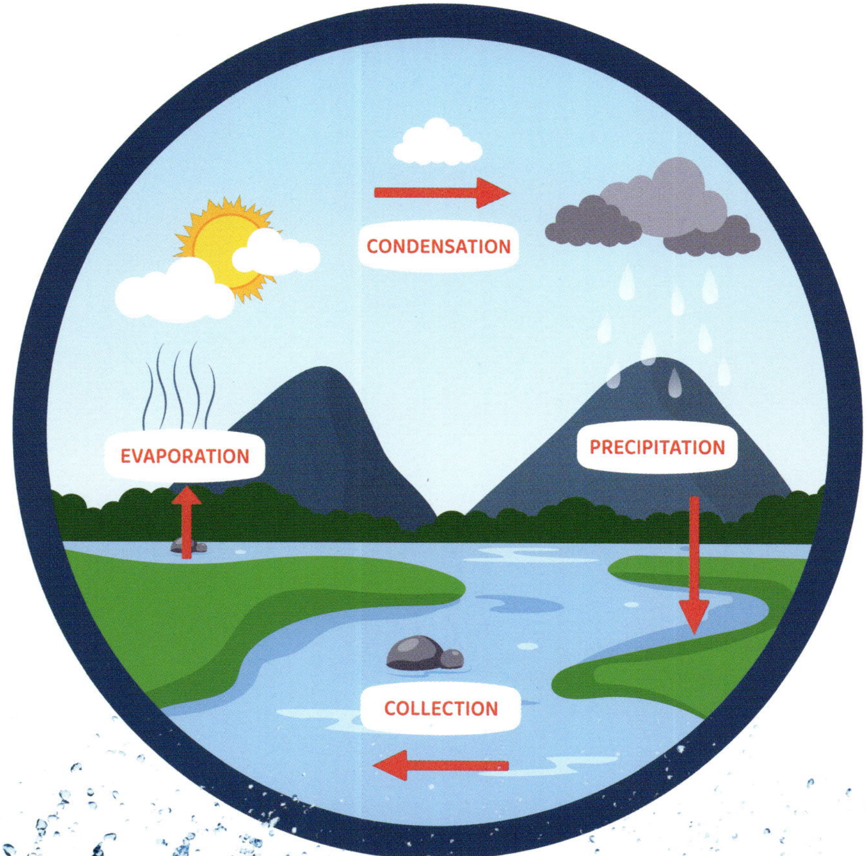

Glossary

collection (kuh-LEK-shuhn): gathering together from different places

condensation (kahn-den-SAY-shuhn): the changing of a gas or vapor into a liquid form

cycle (SYE-kuhl): a series of events that repeat over and over in the same order

evaporation (i-vap-uh-RAY-shuhn): the changing of a liquid into a gas or vapor

hail (hayl): small balls of ice that fall from clouds

precipitation (pri-sip-i-TAY-shuhn): the falling of water from the sky in the form of rain, sleet, hail, or snow

sleet (sleet): frozen or partially frozen rain; a mixture of rain and snow

water vapor (WAW-tur VAY-pur): water in the state of a gas; tiny, invisible water droplets

Thinking Questions

1. What is evaporation?
2. When does water fall from clouds?
3. Why does most rain begin as snow?
4. Name and describe different kinds of precipitation.
5. Does Earth ever make new water? Why or why not?

Index

About the Author

A.B. Clamant is the author of several fact-filled books for kids. The daughter of two grade school teachers, she developed a love of children's books at an early age. When she's not writing, she is working on opening her own petting zoo, ABCs Animals. Her favorite foods are bread, fruit strips, and candy. A.B. Clamant lives in Springfield, Missouri, with her four cats: Monkey, Corky, Prissy, and Nelly.